A FIRST LOOK AT AMERICA'S PRESIDENTS

THOMAS JEFFERSON

The 3rd President

by Josh Gregory

Consultant: Meena Bose
Director, Peter S. Kalikow Center for the Study of the American Presidency
Peter S. Kalikow Chair in Presidential Studies
Professor, Political Science
Hofstra University
Hempstead, New York

BEARPORT
PUBLISHING

New York, New York
CHILDREN'S LIBRARY

Credits

Cover, © Alliance Images/Alamy; 4, © Don Fink/Shutterstock; 5, © dbimages/Alamy; 6, © Steve Heap/
Shutterstock; 7, © Florin Burlan/Shutterstock; 8–9, © North Wind Picture Archives/Alamy; 10, Courtesy
of the Library of Congress; 11, Courtesy of the Library of Congress; 12, U.S. Navy/Wikimedia Commons/
Public Domain; 13, © Stocktrek Images, Inc./Alamy; 14, Courtesy of the Library of Congress; 15, © GL Archive/
Alamy; 17T, © Bettmann/Corbis/AP Images; 17B, © Jason Patrick Ross/Shutterstock; 18, Courtesy of the Library
of Congress; 19, Courtesy of the Library of Congress; 20, © Lebrecht Music and Arts Photo Library/Alamy;
21TL, © Stocktrek Images, Inc./Alamy; 21TR, Courtesy of the Library of Congress; 21B, © Bettmann/Corbis/AP
Images; 22, Courtesy of the Library of Congress; 23, Courtesy of the Library of Congress.

Publisher: Kenn Goin
Editor: Joyce Tavolacci
Creative Director: Spencer Brinker
Design: The Design Lab
Photo Researcher: Jennifer Zeiger

Special thanks to fifth-grader Lucy Barr and second-grader Brian Barr for their help in reviewing this book.

Library of Congress Cataloging-in-Publication Data

Gregory, Josh.
  Thomas Jefferson : the 3rd President / by Josh Gregory.
      pages cm—(A first look at America's Presidents)
  Includes bibliographical references and index.
  ISBN 978-1-62724-553-1 (library binding : alk. paper)—ISBN 1-62724-553-7 (library binding : alk. paper)
  1. Jefferson, Thomas, 1743–1826—Juvenile literature. 2. Presidents—United States—Biography—Juvenile literature.
  I. Title.
  E332.79.G76 2015
  973.4'6092—dc23
  [B]
                                      2014035731

For more information, write to Bearport Publishing Company, Inc., 45 West 21st Street, Suite 3B,
New York, New York 10010. Printed in the United States of America.

10 9 8 7 6 5 4 3 2 1

CONTENTS

Leading the Way **4**

A Serious Student **6**

War and Freedom **8**

An Important Document **10**

The New Government **12**

President Jefferson **14**

The Country Grows **16**

Heading Home **18**

Timeline 20

Facts and Quotes 22

Glossary 23

Index 24

Read More 24

Learn More Online 24

About the Author 24

Leading the Way

Thomas Jefferson was one of the most important Americans of his time. First, as a thinker and writer, he helped shape America's laws and government. Later, as president, he doubled the size of the United States.

Jefferson bought land from France, increasing the size of the United States.

Thomas Jefferson was the third president. He served from 1801 to 1809.

A Serious Student

Thomas Jefferson was born in 1743 in the **colony** of Virginia. As a child, Thomas loved to learn. He often studied up to 15 hours a day. Later, Thomas became a lawyer.

Thomas went to the College of William & Mary.

Part of MA

Claimed by NY and NH

NH
NY
MA
RI
PA
CT
NJ
Virginia
DE
MD
NC
SC
GA

Atlantic Ocean

N
W E
S

13 American Colonies

In the 1700s, there were 13 American colonies. The colonies were ruled by Great Britain.

Thomas also loved music. He played the violin.

War and Freedom

In the 1770s, unfair British laws and high **taxes** made Jefferson and many other Americans angry. Jefferson spoke and wrote about ending British rule. In 1775, Americans went to war against Britain to win their freedom.

The war was called the Revolutionary War.

9

An Important Document

In 1776, Jefferson met with other American leaders in Pennsylvania. They decided to put into words what America was fighting for. Jefferson **drafted** the **text**. It said that all people have the right to be free. It also said that America should be its own country.

The important text was called the Declaration of Independence. It took 18 days to write.

Jefferson

Benjamin Franklin (left), John Adams (center), and Jefferson work on the Declaration of Independence.

The Revolutionary War ended in 1783. The colonies won the war.

The New Government

After the war, the colonies were a new country called the United States. Jefferson helped lead the new government. He became the first secretary of state in 1790. In this job, he worked with leaders of other countries. Then, in 1796, he became vice president.

Jefferson served as vice president under President John Adams (above).

Jefferson knew six languages. They were English, Italian, Spanish, French, Greek, and Latin. The languages, especially French, helped him as secretary of state.

Jefferson loved to travel. He especially loved France and Italy.

13

President Jefferson

In 1800, Jefferson was **elected** president. He worked hard to make sure the government was not too powerful. He did not want it to be like the British government. He wanted to protect people's right to speak freely.

Jefferson was a very popular president. Most Americans liked the way he led the country.

As president, Jefferson sent the U.S. Navy to fight pirates in the Mediterranean Sea. The navy won the battle.

The Country Grows

In 1803, Jefferson doubled the size of the country. He bought a huge piece of land from France. It was called the Louisiana Territory. Much of the land was unexplored. Jefferson sent people to map it.

In 1804, Jefferson ran for president again and won.

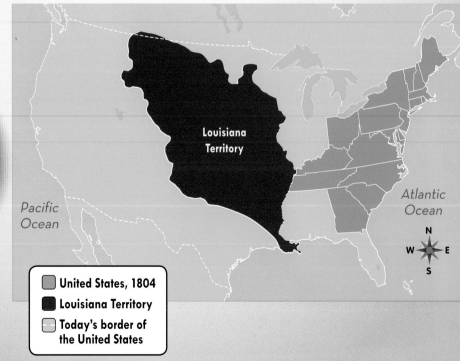

Louisiana Territory

Pacific Ocean

Atlantic Ocean

N
W E
S

■ United States, 1804
■ Louisiana Territory
□ Today's border of the United States

Part of the
Louisiana Territory

Jefferson sent Meriwether
Lewis and William Clark to
explore the Louisiana Territory.

Heading Home

Jefferson left office in 1809. Then he went to his home in Virginia. He read books and spent time with his family. Then, at age 83, he died there. Today, he is remembered as a leader whose great ideas helped shape America.

The Jefferson Memorial opened on April 13, 1943. That would have been Jefferson's 200th birthday.

The Jefferson Memorial is in Washington, D.C.

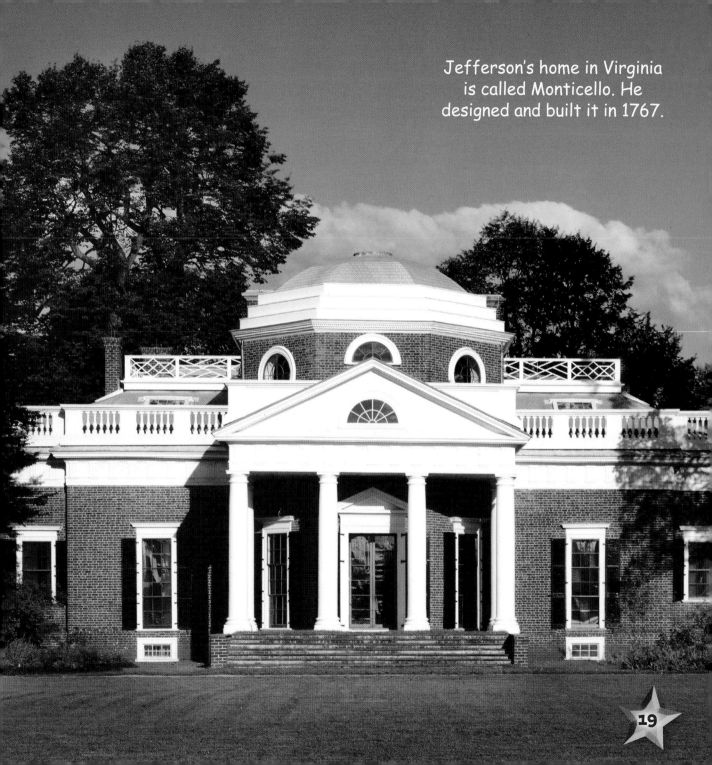

Jefferson's home in Virginia is called Monticello. He designed and built it in 1767.

TIMELINE

Here are some major events from Thomas Jefferson's life.

1775–1783
The American colonies battle Great Britain in the Revolutionary War.

1743
Jefferson is born in the colony of Virginia.

1762
Jefferson graduates from college.

| 1740 | 1750 | 1760 | 1770 | 1780 |

1776
Jefferson drafts the Declaration of Independence.

1800
Jefferson is elected president.

1803
The United States buys the Louisiana Territory from France.

1826
Jefferson dies at his home, Monticello.

1790 · 1800 · 1810 · 1820 · 1830

1790
President George Washington chooses Jefferson as the first secretary of state.

1804
Jefferson sends Lewis and Clark to explore the Louisiana Territory. Jefferson is re-elected president.

FACTS and QUOTES

"I cannot live without books."

Jefferson was also an inventor. He invented a plow and a tiny desk.

Jefferson helped build and start the University of Virginia.

"We hold these truths to be self-evident, that all men are created equal."

Jefferson died exactly 50 years after the signing of the Declaration of Independence. John Adams died the same day.

In 1772, Jefferson married Martha Wayles Skelton. She died just ten years later. They had six children. Two daughters, Martha and Maria, lived to be adults.

THOMAS JEFFERSON

GLOSSARY

13 American Colonies

colony (KOL-uh-nee) an area that has been settled by people from another country and is ruled by that country

Declaration of Independence (dek-luh-RAY-shuhn UV in-di-PEN-duhnss) a text signed by American leaders on July 4, 1776, that declared the freedom of the 13 American colonies from British rule

drafted (DRAFT-id) prepared an early version of a text

elected (i-LEK-tihd) chosen by vote

memorial (muh-MOR-ee-uhl) a statue or other object made to help people remember someone

taxes (TAKS-iz) money paid by people to the ruler or government of a country

text (TEKST) a written work

Index

Adams, John 10, 12, 22
birth 6, 20
childhood 6
colonies 6–7, 11, 12, 20
death 18, 21, 22
Declaration of
    Independence 10–11,
    20, 22
education 6–7, 13, 22

France 4, 13, 16
Franklin, Benjamin 10
Great Britain 7, 8, 14,
    20
Jefferson Memorial 18
Lewis and Clark
    Expedition 17, 21
Louisiana Territory 4,
    16–17, 21

marriage 22
Monticello 18–19, 21
Revolutionary War 8–9,
    11, 20
U.S. Navy 15
Virginia 6–7, 18–19,
    20, 22
years in office 5

Read More

Gosman, Gillian. *Thomas Jefferson (Life Stories).* New York: PowerKids Press (2011).

Jurmain, Suzanne. *Worst of Friends: Thomas Jefferson, John Adams, and the True Story of an American Feud.* New York: Dutton (2011).

Kalman, Maira. *Thomas Jefferson: Life, Liberty and the Pursuit of Everything.* New York: Nancy Paulsen Books (2014).

Learn More Online

To learn more about Thomas Jefferson, visit **www.bearportpublishing.com/AmericasPresidents**

About the Author:
Josh Gregory writes and edits books for kids. He lives in Chicago, Illinois.

24